And the Women Came First

by
Sabrina J. Ellis

Acknowledgments

I am forever grateful to God for a husband who acknowledges, supports and defends women in ministry. Bishop J. Delano Ellis II is not only my husband; but he is the father of my children, my pastor and my greatest fan. Thank you, Honey!

I am thankful for all my sisters in ministry, but specifically: Toni Alvarado, Wanda Parker, Courtney Jenkins, Tameaka Reid, Carolyn Hurst, Michelle Humphrey, Gloria Chaney, Renae Moore and Mila Cooper.

Because of trailblazers like Co-Pastor Susie Owens, Dr. Renita Weems, Dr. Elaine Flake, Dr. Cynthia Hale, Dr. Claudette Copeland, Joann Browning, Dr. Jessica Ingram and Dr. Carolyn Showell; I have a future! Thank you!

FOREWORD

" *A* nd the Women Came First" is more than the title of this much needed new book by Dr. Sabrina Ellis, it is also a reminder that the women who followed Jesus both to the cross and to the tomb were the first persons to announce that Jesus had been raised from the dead. The apostle Paul declares that if Christ is not risen from the dead, than the whole message of Christianity collapses into irrelevance. (Paraphrase, 2 Corinthians 15) Sabrina Ellis bravely and boldly reminds the church, both men and women that the first Christian sermon in the post-resurrection era was delivered by women who went from being the bearers of burial spices to being the very first heralds of the Good News about Jesus Christ.

There are still people in the 21st century trying to make the case that women should not, indeed could never be called to preach the gospel. They argue that because all of the 12 disciples of Jesus were male that means that all persons who stand to preach must also be male. Of course, all 12 of them were also Jewish males who had been circumcised and confined themselves to a kosher diet. I do not see that fact being used to determine which men are authorized or qualified to preach. This book will help the church edge its way into the 21st century on the topic of women in ministry and women as preachers. Women are being called into the ministry by God. They are being called upon to serve as bishops, evangelists, pastors and theological professors. This is as it should be since *And the Women Came First*.

This foreword is a blessing to write for two reasons. First, Dr. Ellis has been my student, my colleague and my friend for over 15 years. Second, she and this book remind me that my first pastor - the first preaching voice I heard as a child was that of The Rev. Mary G.Evans of

Cosmopolitan Community Church of Chicago, Illinois. Anyone who heard Pastor Evans preach then or who reads the inspiring words and testimony of Pastor Ellis now will quickly move beyond the artificial limits that many churches and preachers have sought to impose upon women who seek to follow their calling into the preaching ministry. I invite those who read this book and who then recommend it to others to celebrate and remember this one simple fact in the history of the early Christian community; *And the Women Came First.*

DR. MARVIN MCMICKLE
PRESIDENT
PROFESSOR OF CHURCH LEADERSHIP
COLGATE ROCHESTER CROZER DIVINITY SCHOOL

Introduction

The declaration, *And The Women Came First*, is in no way an indictment against our beloved counterparts. Nor is it an attempt to argue for some kind of position or title in ministry. But it is with deliberation and determination, a presentation for the purpose of stating a fact.

A fact is something known to be true, it is the truth, or reality of something. A fact is a piece of information, an actual course of events; something based on evidence. I have one purpose in mind for writing this book, and that is to state what is true.

Of course, there may be those who will say that what I have written is subjective in nature, suggesting that this is just my perception or observation. However, I will present what the

Bible says as it relates to the women who first preached the Gospel. There are four accounts of the same event in the Scriptures. One mention would have been significant. But to find the same account in all four Gospels suggests that the Apostles Matthew, Mark, Luke and John each thought it worthy enough to write the event into the history of the church (See Matthew 28:1-8, Mark 16:1-8, Luke 24:1-11, John 20:1-2, 11-18). Surely, there is some meaning for us to gather from these passages.

Each apostle writes his account from his own perspective, providing the reader with the necessary information for harmonizing the texts. Matthew mentions *Mary Magdalene and the other Mary* arriving at the tomb of Jesus. He also points out that there was an *earthquake when an angel of the Lord descended from heaven, and came and rolled back the stone from the door, and sat on it.* (See Matthew 28:1-2) Mark informs us that "the other Mary" was the mother of James, but he also includes Salome in his passage (See Mark 16:1). Luke includes Joanna in his story (See Luke 16:10);

while John makes it known that he was with Peter when Mary Magdalene reported to them that Jesus had been taken from the tomb (See Luke 20:2). In the Gospel of John, we also hear Jesus speaking directly to Mary Magdalene, *Mary!* . . . *"Do not cling to Me, for I have not yet ascended to My Father; but go to My brethren and say to them, I am ascending to My Father and your Father, and to My God and your God.* (John 20:17)

There is agreement in the Gospels regarding the distinction of women in this event as the first ones who received news of the Resurrection. After receiving the news, they were instructed to tell the disciples.

Unfortunately, in the 21st century, the Church still struggles with the notion of women in ministry. Despite the many successful female pastors; preachers, bishops, rabbis and chaplains, there are women in ministry who are still rejected or intentionally marginalized. The argument for this resistance is usually one passage found in Paul's writings to the Corinthians.

Paul instructs, *Let your women keep silent in the churches, for they are not permitted to speak; but they are to be submissive, as the law also says.* (I Corinthians 14:34) This was Paul's directive to a disorderly Corinthian church. In addition, he references the law, which suggests that he was teaching the Gentiles a Jewish custom as it related to how a local congregation was to behave. This defense stands on the words of Jesus Christ himself and is an attempt to encourage the woman who has ministry and purpose to respond to her calling.

After receiving their instructions, the women *went out quickly from the tomb with fear and great joy . . . .* (See Matthew 28:8). They were afraid but did not allow their fear to keep them from doing what they were told to do. The awesomeness of the call can be overwhelming and possibly may even lead to fear; yet there is a responsibility to respond to the call. The prospect of not being believed or received can also be frightening; yet the obligation to "Go" is greater.

Table of Contents

Chapter One

God Said Go

*Matthew 28:1-8, Mark 16:1-8, Luke 24:1-11,
John 20:1-2, 11-18*

When we harmonize the New Testament texts in the four Gospels, we find that there were at least four women at the tomb; Mary Magdalene, Mary, the mother of James, Salome, and Joanna. These women went to anoint the body of Jesus with spices. Their intention was either to show additional honor and respect, or out of necessity to finalize the embalming process. Joseph of Arimathea and Nicodemus had already taken the body of Jesus, and wrapped it with spices and strips of linen according to the custom. (See John 19:38-40) These women were going to anoint the body of Jesus out of their love for Him, but also because they did not expect Him to rise in three days.

Who were these women? What roles did they have in the life of Jesus? We know that they were His disciples. They joined the twelve and followed Jesus. Luke 8:3 confirms for us that they were also known to support Him and His ministry financially. But there is more. Let's listen to *them* as they speak to us from the tomb . . . .

Mary Magdalene came from an affluent city near the Sea of Galilee. The city of Magdala is noted for its wealth and immorality. It is plausible to say that Mary Magdalene indulged in the immorality at some point, due to her history. However, she has been mischaracterized as a prostitute. Although history tells us that the city of Mary's nativity was known for and destroyed because of its prostitution, there is no record of her indulging in that particular behavior. What the Bible tells us is that her imperfection was the result of the possession of seven demons. She was controlled by spirits that erased her memory and personality. She suffered convulsions and fits, even fainting; as if she were dying. More than likely, she could be found on many occasions terrorizing her community as she wailed through the streets of Magdala in agony. She was possessed. No doubt, Mary's daily environment influenced her behavior. She probably hung out with the wrong crowd, which would have easily led her to a struggle with good and evil.

But at some point in Mary's life, she changed her companionship. She ended up with women who, like her, were delivered from *evil spirits and infirmities*. (See Luke 8:2) Mary and these other women followed Jesus and supported His ministry, and they were *there looking on from afar* when Jesus was crucified. (See Matthew 27:55) Although it appeared that Jesus hung helplessly on the cross, Mary Magdalene knew firsthand that He had power. And so, because of her love for Him, she was at the tomb that morning with her sisters. (Mark 16:1)

Mary Magdalene still lives among us today. She is that woman that has been oppressed by the evil spirits of the dark kingdom. She is that woman whose environment has negatively influenced her lifestyle, and caused her to live in a downward spiral of negative behavior. Mary Magdalene is that woman who has not only caused harm to others, but has brought harm to herself.

She is the woman who is full of hatred and projects her displaced anger onto innocent and unaware family and friends. She keeps others at a distance with her distastefulness and appears to shy away from relationships. The average person avoids contact with "Mary Magdalene," and warns others that she is a dangerous person. So now, this woman is bitter not only because of her unrelenting negative environment, but the inability for anyone to recognize that she is a prisoner of circumstances. No one has ever made an attempt to unlock the door of her misery and help her to freedom. There hasn't been a friend, a pastor, or even a believer who extended a hand to help pull her out of her pit.

How many women do you know that have a past that has caused so much pain and damage that only God could turn their lives around? Maybe you are that woman? Had it not been for your Savior, you (or they) would have been lost forever. But the goodness and love of Christ makes it possible for us to have an abundant life, despite the past! When Christ comes in contact with our miserable lives, it is as if He erases everything and sets us up for ministry. That is what happened to Mary Magdalene! She had much to be thankful for. This woman loved her Savior so much that she followed Him all the way to His death. Her commitment was sure. Don't you think Jesus knew that?

Mary, the mother of James, is believed to be the wife of Cleophas. Commentaries also suggest that she is related to Mary, the mother of Jesus. There isn't much of anything said in Scripture about her. She doesn't have much of a story or a past to tell, even though she may be a part of Jesus' family. She hasn't done anything significant enough to make it into the history books, except that she watched from a distance as Jesus was brutally beaten and hung on a tree. She too, was at the tomb the morning of the resurrection to anoint His body. Mary, the mother of James is that woman who has been in what appears to be obscurity. No one really knows who she is or where she comes from. She hasn't done anything to draw attention to herself. She isn't known for any major accomplishments.

This woman made herself content with the life she had. She didn't expect anything more. This is the woman that had never achieved status or recognition in elite circles. Neither she, nor her family was well connected in the community. Yet, she had purpose. She did not exist by accident, and she only came to realize her purpose as she followed Jesus. Maybe you recognize her. She is the one least likely to succeed; because she is shy, quiet, and not confrontational. But that day at the tomb, she was among the women who were given one of the greatest assignments that could be given, "Go tell My brethren . . ." Her unassuming ministry emerged from being at the right place at the right time. Could it be that her ministry was to serve in the background until Jesus called her to the foreground?

Salome was also one of the four women who went to the tomb on Resurrection Day. Salome was the wife of Zebedee and the mother of two sons named James and John. James and John walked with Jesus and listened to His teachings; they were invited into the inner circle along with Simon Peter. The three men were led to a high mountain where they witnessed Jesus' transfiguration. Salome's sons saw His face appear like the sun, and His clothes become like light. They were there when Moses and Elijah appeared.

As a result of all that James and John heard and witnessed as they walked with Jesus, Salome came to believe that Jesus was the Messiah. She began to follow Him too. Unfortunately, she did not understand all that the Messiah had spoken to the men during the times of impartation. This was evident when she asked for special seats for her two sons in the kingdom that she thought would be established on earth. Misguided ambition blinded Salome. She did not consider what God intended for her or her sons, but only what she wanted.

The Salomes of today can be found in one of two categories. One category is that Salome was not thinking of herself, and was putting her family first. Solomon 1:6 speaks of the woman who takes care of everyone else and neglects to take care of herself. This is the woman who works hard to make sure everyone has a place at the table, but she stands or goes to another room. This is the woman who spends her time and resources to make others look good; and discounts her role in the process.

The second category is that Salome did not understand what Jesus wanted for her or her sons, and she behaved as if she knew what was best. Jesus revealed Himself to her sons and invited *them* into His inner circle. Jesus had chosen *them*. He told *them* to follow Him. Salome mishandled Jesus' trust by taking an opportunity to ask for exalted positions. This is the woman who seeks after grandiose positions and titles instead of seeking after God and allowing Him to make the promotions. This is the woman who assumes that it is better to be in an exalted place than a place of humility. Salome's spirit is alive and well!

Finally, there is Joanna. Joanna was a woman of wealth and high social ranking in Herod's court because her husband held a prestigious position. She was aware that Herod mocked Jesus prior to His execution. But Joanna's allegiance was with the One who healed her. You see, Joanna had been among the group of women who were healed of evil spirits and infirmities (See Luke 8:2-3). She had also supported Jesus' ministry out of her own financial means.

Joanna recognized that she was free from her malady because of Christ. Neither her husband, nor Herod could do for her what Jesus had done. She took an enormous risk to walk with Him and to support His ministry, but it was worth it. In gratitude, she made it her business to be at the tomb at sunrise on Resurrection Day.

Here we have the woman who has everything at her disposal. She wants for nothing. Not only does she have the means for purchasing whatever her heart desires, but she is also well connected. She is recognized as someone of importance and could very likely use her power to command whatever she desired. But, she knew with all of the prestige and power, she could not heal herself of her demons. Whatever misery she experienced, her only hope was in Christ.

The Joanna's in the world are the women who have accomplished much. These ladies are connected to powerful people. They seldom want for material things because most of those things are readily available. However, these ladies often deal with secret pain. Something is going on emotionally that they cannot talk about. These women are seen as having everything a woman would want, and because of that, no one recognizes the pain. Joanna hears the voices of others saying, "She is wealthy, she can have whatever she wants!" She hears others saying, "Her husband has a high position in the political arena, she gets to go where she wants!" It is assumed that all is well because of her position and her possessions. But in reality, demons torment her and she longs for deliverance from an emotional prison. Have you met any Joanna's?

Joanna has deeply embedded painful emotions that remain hidden from the public. She is successful at keeping up the part of herself that she reveals to the public, which is a small percent of who she really is. She puts her mask on faithfully each day and attempts to face the world in hopes that "the world" will not see the real her.

These are the women who came first! They were women with problems and concerns. They were women with families. They were women whose lives were not perfect. They were women who had needs.

They were women who experienced emotional and spiritual challenges. Each of these women came from different backgrounds and they had different experiences, none of which kept them from being at the tomb where Jesus had been buried. They loved Him. He had given them what they needed for their journey. They had walked with Him. They had supported His ministry. They were at the cross and witnessed Him being tortured and murdered. Their love for Jesus caused them to be concerned for Him, even after death.

So, Mary Magdalene, Mary, the mother of James, Salome and Joanna decided to go to His tomb. To their surprise, when they got there; He was gone. They had prepared themselves to anoint His body, but He was not there. How frightening that must have been for them! They expected to find the body of Jesus in the tomb where He had been laid. So, where could his body be? As they pondered what they saw, an angel answered their concerns. The Bible said he told them, *Do not be alarmed. You seek Jesus of Nazareth, who was crucified. He is risen! He is not here. See the place where they laid Him.* (Mark 16:6) After the angel gave them the privilege of looking at the place where Jesus laid, he commanded them to go quickly and tell His disciples that He is risen from the dead. (See Mark 16:6)

How exciting that God's plan included these four women! God could have arranged for Peter to be at the tomb first. He could have arranged for the disciples to be present on Resurrection morning, but He chose to have these women there before anyone else. He arranged it so that the women would be the first to see that

He was not in the tomb. They were the first to hear that He had risen. And they were the first to spread the good news (the gospel). God planned it so that the Great Commission was not given to the eleven disciples until after He had commissioned the women. The women were told to "Go", before the disciples were told to "Go" (See Matthew 28:10).

Mary Magdalene was possessed with seven demons and she had had a bad reputation because of where she came from, but she was delivered and God said GO! Mary, the mother of James didn't have a big name or a major role in society. She might have even been considered insignificant in the scheme of things. In these contemporary times, Mary would probably be considered a "nobody", but God said GO!

Salome became full of pride and misguided ambition because her sons had a special place in Jesus' circle, but God said GO! Joanna had money and prestige. She was a part of the King's court that set out to embarrass Jesus and make Him look like a criminal, but God told her to GO! Go and tell my disciples that I have risen!

Reflection

Do I identify with any of these women? If so, in what way?

_____

_____

_____

_____

What is the before and after story of these women?

_____

_____

_____

_____

What is my before and after story?

_____

_____

_____

_____

Prayer: *Lord thank you for reminding me that you are my healer and deliverer. Thank you for qualifying me for ministry and giving me the "Go" to declare your word. Please grant me wisdom and knowledge for effective ministry.*

Chapter Two

A Chance to Make it Right

"For if there is first a willing mind, it is accepted according to what one has, and not according to what he does not have."
2 Corinthians 8:12

The commission to "Go" is not about competing with our male counterparts. It is not about proving that we have a special calling on our lives. Rather, it is about proving our obedience to the One who gave the commandment. From the beginning, man was commanded to obey God. In the Garden of Eden, God commanded Adam (the first man) not to eat of the tree of knowledge of good and evil (See Genesis 2:17). Eve (the first woman) eats the fruit of the forbidden tree after being misguided by a serpent in the garden (See Genesis 3:1-6). Because Eve has not had any experience with deceit, she believes the serpent and makes the wrong choice.

I believe that by sending the four women who were at the tomb to announce His resurrection, Jesus was providing an opportunity for women to fulfill God's original intention and purpose. From the beginning, God intended for man and woman to be his representatives in the earth. He created male and female in His image (See Genesis 1:27). He blessed both of them and told them to "fill the earth and subdue it" (See Genesis 1:28). God intended for man and woman together to have dominion over the earth and to be dwelling places for Him. His intent was not for woman to be excluded from the glory that would be revealed through man and woman's combined expression. But Eve was deceived.

There have been many discussions and debates why Eve ended up doing exactly what God had commanded Adam not to do. Most of the discussion is speculation, in my opinion.

Eve has been blamed for causing the curse on all of mankind, and Adam is seen as one who attempted to avoid any blame by pointing his finger at Eve. (See Genesis 3:12) But, whatever one thinks, the scripture clearly states that, *the serpent was more cunning than any beast of the field.* (See Genesis 3:1) Neither Adam, nor Eve, had ever experienced such crafty, calculating, and scheming behavior. Eve was approached by a serpent that successfully deceived her into going against God's plan for mankind. Eve's desire for knowledge and the serpent's ability to convince her that God was keeping something from her, led to the schism between God and man.

Although God's instructions not to eat of the tree of the knowledge of good and evil were given to Adam, Eve knew of the command. (See Genesis 3:1-3) Eve's initial responses to the serpent were certainly innocent, but not exactly as the instructions had been given. Genesis 2:16-17 says, *And the Lord God commanded the man saying, of every tree of the garden you may freely eat; but of the tree of the knowledge of good and evil you shall not eat, for in the day that you eat of it you shall surely die.* But when the serpent asked Eve if God had really said they could not eat of the trees of the garden, she attempted to explain what was permitted and what wasn't. She told the serpent that she and Adam could *eat the fruit of the trees of the garden, but of the fruit of the tree which is in the midst of the garden, God has said, you shall not eat it, nor shall you touch it, lest you die.* (Genesis 3:2-3) Eve changes what God said in Chapter 2 of Genesis. Instead of her referring to the forbidden tree by what it was, she referred to it by location. She changed "tree of the knowledge of good and evil" to "tree which is in the midst of the garden". Eve also added the phrase, *you shall not touch it.* (Genesis 3:3) Even though Eve misrepresented God's instructions, she did get the last part right; *lest you die!* (Genesis 3:3)

Unfortunately, Eve was misled and listened to the voice of reasoning and deception. The serpent convinced her that she would not really die, but instead she would be as knowledgeable as God. What a temptation! To be like God, knowing good and evil was appealing to Eve, so she disregarded what God had said and surrendered to the desire to know. But God gave us an opportunity to rectify Eve's error!

The women at the tomb were given specific instructions. They were given the privilege of being the first to tell about the resurrection! The women were trusted to carry the gospel! That cannot be disputed! The angel at the tomb said, *Go quickly and tell His disciples that He is risen from the dead....* (Matthew 28:7) How powerful! After the first woman had committed such a major blunder in the beginning, God gave women a chance to make it right!

Eve died with the stigma of disobedience. The women who were first at the tomb and commanded to "Go" will forever be remembered with the honor of obedience. How will you be remembered? The woman who stepped out in obedience, or the woman who succumbed to disobedience?

Unfortunately, many see Eve's disobedience as a reason to denounce women in ministry.

Women see themselves as not being worthy of such a calling, while men use it as a reminder that women "messed up" from the beginning. My response is, *For sin shall not have dominion over you, for you are not under law but under grace.* (Romans 6:14) We live in the age of the New Covenant, where God forgives and forgets sin. Hebrews 9:15 says, *And for this reason He is the Mediator of the new covenant, by means of death for the redemption of the trans-gressions under the first covenant, that those who are called may receive the promise of the eternal inheritance.* Therefore, even if women did "mess up" from the beginning, the New Covenant is in effect because Christ died!

Reflection

Can you recall a time you were made to feel like you weren't good enough because of your mistakes? When and where was it?

_____

_____

_____

_____

In what way has God given you a second chance?

_____

_____

_____

_____

Prayer: *Thank you God, for a second chance. Thank you for forgiveness and an opportunity to serve. Give me grace to do what you have called me to do. With your grace, I will honor you with my obedience.*

Chapter Three

What if Some Don't Believe?

*If you persist in staying silent at a time like this,
help and deliverance will arrive for the Jews
from someplace else; but you and your family
will be wiped out. Who knows? Maybe you
were made queen for just such a time as this.*
_____*Esther 4:14 (MSG)*

The disciples did not believe the women when they reported that Jesus had risen and that they had seen him. Luke 24:11 says, *And their words seemed to them like idle tales, and they did not believe them.* However, the Gospel of Mark reveals that Jesus personally rebuked the disciples for not believing the women. The Gospel of Mark recorded, *Later He appeared to the eleven as they sat at the table; and He rebuked their unbelief and hardness of heart, because they did not believe those who had seen Him after He had risen.* (Mark 16:14)

Everyone is not going to believe a woman is called or sent to preach. Everyone is not going to trust the word that comes from the mouth of a woman. Some believe it's a man's job. Some just don't believe. Others misinterpret Paul's message to Corinthian women in I Corinthians 14:34. *Let your women keep silent in the churches, for they are not permitted to speak; but they are to be submissive, as the law also says.* (I Corinthians 14:34) But Bishop Vashti McKenzie said in her book entitled *Not Without A Struggle,* "Whenever belief systems are challenged, no amount of evidence, biblical or otherwise, will ever be enough for some people. It will be what you do, not what you say that counts."

There have also been other women who have made it difficult for those of us who have a word and an anointing from the Lord. Unfortunately, those women who do not support women in ministry have been influenced to believe that a woman's place cannot rise above taking care of her husband and/or her children. I am familiar with one church that will not permit a woman to step up to the pulpit area for any reason, not even to serve the preacher. There was a time that I was invited to speak at a women's event, but I was told I would be ministering from the podium on the floor. Another women's organization I know of would rather keep women at the missionary level because of financial reports: if a woman is listed as a minister or elder; her report no longer boosts the income for the women's organization, but is redirected to another group.

The resistance to women in ministry is found as frequently among women as it is among men. In addition to their interpretation (or misinterpretation) of Scripture; women often display resentment and jealousy for women in ministry. I have found in one particular organization, while men are debating the issue of ordaining women; the women are uninterested and present no defense or justification for ordination. Could it be that they have been marginalized for so long that they are comfortable where they are? In many cases, the women themselves do not feel worthy of such an elevation. Self-esteem plays a major role here.

Whatever the case may be, much time and effort is wasted trying to correct all of the misunderstandings and misinterpretations of Scripture concerning a woman's place in the church. I will admit that it can be an uphill battle at times, but knowing that you were called and "who" called you should provide you with the necessary energy for the fight. The assurance that you have been given a mandate from God to fulfill His purpose must carry more weight than the skepticism of the unknowing.

When we consider that souls are lost and dying, and that we have the message that can and will save them, we need to be about our Father's business. We must be intentional about which unbelievers we are seeking to convince. The unbeliever that does not know Christ is a soul that could possibly be lost, while we are trying to convince the person who doesn't believe in women in ministry. God has called you for a specific purpose and you cannot afford to ignore that calling because of someone else's fears. However, should you choose not to respond to your call, the job will get done! That was the sum of Mordecai's message to Esther in the Book of Esther. Mordecai spoke to Esther saying, *For if you remain silent at this time, relief and deliverance for the Jews will arise from another place, but you and your father's family will perish. And who knows but that you have come to your royal position for such a time as this?* (Esther 4:14)

The Apostle Luke lets us know that the disciples did not believe the women (See Luke 24:11). Although Peter was among those who did not believe, he jumped up and ran to the tomb and stooped down to look in. When he realized that there was nobody in the tomb, he left there amazed. (See Luke 24:12) But it gets better! The following verses tell us that two of the disciples were walking along the road and talking about all that had happened. Jesus walked with them, but they did not know who He was. According to the text, they did not recognize Jesus until after He had sat down and ate with them and then disappeared. After the disciples realized that Jesus was actually alive and not just missing from his tomb, they said, *The Lord is risen indeed, and has appeared to Simon!* (Luke 24:13-16, 34)

It seems that the disciples only gave the women partial credit. They admitted that the women were right about Jesus not being in the grave, but the disciples were not sure that meant He was alive, because they had not seen Him. The fact that they had not seen Him, or did not believe the women, did not change the fact that Jesus had gotten up from the grave!

It is not my intention to be argumentative about this issue. My purpose is to empower women who still struggle with not being accepted in their role as preaching women. Don't use your time defending yourself. Just do what you were called to do! You must be confident in who you are and what your assignment is. I will discuss this more in the next chapter, but understanding who you are is critical to doing effective ministry.

Unfortunately, too many women who believe God called them to the ministry are not secure about who they are. I am not unaware of the reality that we live in a patriarchal society. It has been said that this is a man's world! But we do have a significant role, not just in the world, but also in the Body of Christ. We got another chance! God has given us the opportunity to make it right!

God intended from the beginning for man and woman to express His glory. That combined expression was interrupted when a woman was deceived. It started with the tree of knowledge and good and evil. But it ended with another tree! It ended at the cross! Because of the cross, we have a gospel to preach!

As a final statement for this chapter, I would like to again address I Corinthians 14:34. This passage is often used to defend the argument against preaching women. Fortunately for women, it is not as cut and dry as it may seem to those who use the text to disaffirm the ministry of women. In I Corinthians Paul is speaking to a church that has gotten completely out of order. He deals with gifts, prophecies, and tongues and in the latter part of Chapter 14 he deals with church gatherings. Paul was not forbidding women to manifest spiritual gifts, but he was attempting to stop the undisciplined discussions that disrupted the service.

He had already outlined the proper conduct at the Lord's Supper in Chapter 11, and he furthered his resolution of doctrinal and practical problems in the local church by discussing the diversity in the Body of Christ. Paul was dealing with a culture that had been accustomed to gross sexual immorality, idolatry, divisive philosophies and the rejection of the resurrection of Christ. The apostle had to put things in perspective for a people who were used to pagan worship and wild compulsive behavior. In that pagan worship, women were permitted to participate by making loud high-pitched screams called ululations. While the men made sacrifices, the women provided the sound effects. The Apostle Paul had the task of maintaining order in Corinthian worship.

It was not Paul's intention to forever silence women in the Body of Christ. In addition to the possibility of stopping the women from reverting to a type of pagan worship, he was more than likely dealing with an issue of undisciplined discussions that disrupted worship. In addition, women were forbidden to take authority over men (See I Timothy 2:12), but this prohibition does not forbid women to proclaim the truth or exhort. The Apostle Luke wrote in Acts 2:17, *And it shall come to pass in the last days, says God, that I will pour out of My Spirit on all flesh; Your sons and your daughters shall prophesy . . . .* In Acts 18:26, Aquila and Priscilla explained *the way of God more accurately* to Apollos. And in Philippians 4:3, Paul encourages a member of the Philippian church to help two women who *labored with me in the gospel.* Therefore, Paul's overall message to the church at Corinth was to discontinue their pagan-like behavior. The apostle was providing specific guidelines and instructions to a specific church and culture. He was not condemning women in ministry. Paul's objective was decency and order.

Dr. Marvin McMickle, author and president of Colgate Rochester Crozer Divinity School, points out in his book entitled *Deacons in Today's Black Baptist Church*; "Paul did not say a woman should not be permitted to preach in the church; Paul said a woman should not even speak." McMickle goes on to say that, "If this text were to be literally interpreted and applied to the life of every local church, without regard for the original context of the passage or the subsequent shifts in the cultures from the first to the twenty-first century, then women would not be expected to be silent in the pulpit alone; they would be silent everywhere in the church." In other words, if we follow Paul's instruction to the letter, women would have absolutely nothing to say in the church setting. All women in church would listen only; they would not teach, lead committees or groups, or make announcements. If taken literally without consideration for the time in history or the culture, Paul's statement impacts far more than just women preaching.

The interpretations of Paul's writings have guided the way for the teaching about women in the church for as long as I can remember. Clearly, that teaching goes further back into the history of the church than I care to address here, however, it is important to understand how we are impacted when we do not listen for what God intended for the Body. If He had intended for women to be excluded from the ministry of preaching the gospel, He would not have called on the women who were at the tomb first to be the ones to tell of His resurrection.

Whatever Paul needed to address or correct in the Corinthian church, Jesus had already established a precedent when He said to the women in Matthew 28:10, *Do not be afraid, go and tell My brethren to go to Galilee, and there they will see Me.* And God's word to us today is the same, "Don't be afraid, go . . . ." Those words provide for us the reassurance necessary for doing what we have been called to do. Just as Peter heard Jesus speak the word "come" and was able to walk on water (See Matthew 14:29), we have been commanded to "go". It is imperative for us to embrace that one word as the platform on which to stand, without fear, to declare the Word of the Lord.

Finally, the greatest defense for women in ministry is found in Galatians 3:28, *There is neither Jew nor Greek, there is neither slave nor free, there is neither male nor female; for you are all one in Christ Jesus.* There are no nationalities, no classes, or genders in Christ Jesus. All who accept Christ are justified by Him, and become children of God; we are no longer sinners. Paul said, *For you are all sons of God through faith in Christ Jesus.* (Galatians 3:28) There is no inequality.

Paul was making it clear to the Galatians that the social classes that were developing among the Jews and Gentiles were unacceptable. Gentiles were being forced to become Jews in order to be accepted by Jewish Christians. But Paul wanted them to understand that everyone had equal status because of the Gospel. Jews did not have to become Gentiles to participate in the life of the church; neither do women have to become men.

Lack of understanding, misinterpretation of scripture, the inability to affirm others and a number of other issues that other people have cause some women to become discouraged and question the legitimacy of their call. I have personally experienced the discouragement of an "unbeliever", but I decided not to allow it stop me. Instead, it became my springboard.

While working toward my undergraduate degree, I accepted my call to the ministry. I believed that my education would enhance my ministry, and that I would use my major in Psychology to help people. There was a member of my family that I respected very much who did not believe that I would complete my education, or do anything significant where ministry was concerned. To say that I was hurt is a mild description of how I felt. I was disappointed to know that this family member had little to no confidence in me to reach my goal. There may have been others who felt the same, but no one else had been as vocal as this male relative. Periodically, throughout my process of achieving an education and growing in ministry,

I would hear the words, "You won't finish, and you probably won't do any more than what you are doing now." I was almost convinced at one point that I was not cut out for all that ministry and school required. But I remembered that if God had confidence enough in me to call me, He had to have a plan for preparing me and using me. Rather than allow the lack of confidence someone else had in me to stop me, I used it to encourage myself and trust God.

Reflection

Has your confidence ever been shaken because someone did not believe in you? If so, how did you respond?

_____

_____

_____

_____

How has tradition played a role in your call to ministry?

_____

_____

_____

_____

Pray: Lord, help me trust you to use me. Despite discouragement, disbelief and disappointment, strengthen me to stand in the power of your might and to do what you have commanded me to do.

Chapter Four

The Person in the Ministry

"I had been my whole life a bell, and never knew it until at that moment I was lifted and struck."
_____*Annie Dillard*

As supportive as I am of women in the ministry, I am also a proponent of knowing and understanding ones purpose in the ministry. Admittedly, there are those women who have made it difficult for other women in ministry simply because they claimed to be called to something they were never intended to do. The preaching/teaching/pastoral ministry is not for every woman that decides she likes the idea. It is work! And if we are going to put our best foot forward, we need to have a plan. So, while this particular chapter may not necessarily be a continuation of the defense for women in ministry, it does provide essential information to the women I defend.

It is important for us to be clear about who we are, why we are here and what we do best. We need to know our unique mission in life. We need to understand our gifts and talents and what our purpose is in ministry, so we do not end up off course or out of sync with God's plan for us. I have discovered that there are many women who are not confident about their own ministries. There could be several reasons for this. Many women have not matured as it relates to their gifts. Nor have they had the opportunity to sit under the kind of leadership that would develop them. Many times gifts and talents are not recognized (by the individual, or anyone else), in which case they lie dormant. And in some cases, the individual's gifts or talents are not considered traditional enough for the church or ministry an individual is a part of.

It is essential for the person in the ministry to develop a personal philosophy of life and ministry by understanding ones self, ones gift, and ones goal. A personal philosophy may serve as a guide for achieving specific goals in ministry. It provides a portrait of what the ministry looks like, or will look like, and how and where it fits.

Understanding who you are will define your limitations and help you realize the difference between skills and gifts. A skill reflects the ability to do a job, but it does not necessarily mean there is a gift or passion for doing the job. Any teachable person can learn to do something. The question is what are you gifted to do? What gift(s) did God give you? Frustration is the emotional outcome of doing things that are not a good fit. Unfortunately, there are a lot of people who have been trained to do jobs that just don't fit who they are. When we don't understand our gifts and talents and what our purpose is in ministry, we end up misplaced and out of sync with God's plan for us. One of the best examples of this was given in a class I attended nine years ago. The students were given an exercise. Each of us wrote our signatures with our preferred hand. Those who were right handed, signed with their right hand and those who were left handed, signed with their left hand. After that, we were instructed to do the same thing with the opposite hand, the non-preferred hand. We discovered that when one uses a non-preferred function, more time is needed and it feels uncomfortable. The lesson learned was that the person in a ministry that does not suit them has the same reaction as the person using a non-preferred function. It is difficult and takes more time than it normally would if it were a "good fit".

To ensure that you are doing ministry with your "preferred hand", you must consider several things. Who am I? What is my mission? What are my values? And, what is my goal? The answers to these questions guide you through the process of developing your own philosophy of ministry.

A Personal Portrait. The first component to developing a personal philosophy of life and ministry is a personal portrait. This is the answer to the question, "Who am I?" This is where you work to understand your personality and how it impacts those you come in contact with. Your personality is key to what your ministry will look like. Your true personality will not permit you to successfully do what someone else's personality will permit them to do.

Everyday of our lives we do the things we enjoy and we use talents we have, never understanding that these are life gifts that make up who we are. Unfortunately, this is why so many people never reach their potential. After discovering the importance of knowing myself, I was introduced to personality assessments. These assessments confirmed some things I knew about myself and revealed some things I was not aware of. The results of one assessment I took pointed out that my areas of interest are Artistic and Social. Writing, reporting, and technical writing are also qualities that I possess. I love music and have an interest in art. I am not a composer, but I like to design and create. Socially, I enjoy teaching and training others. I take pleasure in organizing social gatherings and facilitating events.

I have also learned my personality type. According to Myers-Briggs (another personality assessment), I am of the introvert intuitive type. My Myers-Briggs four-letter type is INFJ. The characteristics of this type are to succeed by perseverance, originality, and desire to do whatever is needed or wanted. The person of this of this type is to put their best efforts into their work, and is quietly forceful, conscientious, and concerned for others. This person is respected for their firm principles, and is likely to be honored and followed for their clear convictions as to how best to serve the common good. This is a pretty good indication of who I am.

By understanding these insights regarding my interests and my personality type, I was able to better define my spiritual gifts. The authors of a book entitled *LifeKeys* (Kise, Start, and Hirsh, 1996) were instrumental in defining these gifts for me. I won't belabor the point, but I will say that all of the assessments, including a spiritual gifts assessment have been beneficial to developing my own philosophy of life and ministry. Equally as important, the possibility of the temptation to adopt the style and mannerisms of other ministers was avoided.

Through this process, I was able to realize *my* strengths and *my* weaknesses and develop goals and a plan for succeeding. The temptation to look and act like someone else is always prevalent, but authenticity always trumps the temptation. We do not have to preach like our male counterparts to be successful. We do not have to sound like them to be heard. Dr. Marvin McMickle quoted Reverend Gardner Taylor:

> "When we begin to imitate the traits and habits of other preachers we fail twice. The first failure is that we cannot really be like someone else because we have not walked long enough in their shoes. We fail a second time because we fail to be the person God intended or preferred us to be."

I recommend that every woman in ministry do whatever is necessary to answer the "*who am I?*" question. If you don't know where to begin, start with a Christian Counseling Agency in your area. It is worth the investment!

Mission Statement. The second component for developing a philosophy for life and ministry is a mission statement. A clear mission statement that expresses what you will do helps to keep you focused. This statement should sum up your goals and provide guidance for all that you do in ministry. What is your task or assignment? What will you do? This statement should be a brief paragraph, of two to three sentences that reflects your priorities and convictions about the purpose of your life and ministry. By referring to your mission statement periodically, you are able to stay focused.

I have come to realize that it is not enough to talk about what you would like to do. It was not until I developed my own personal philosophy for life and ministry that I took myself seriously. When you take the time to think through *how* your vision or mission will actually come to pass, and then take the time to write it, you are more likely to accomplish the task.

Values. Values are the things that are important to you and define your fundamental character (*LifeKeys*, Kise, Stark, Hirsh 1996, 166).

They supply meaning to your work and life, as well as influence the decisions you make. Values also compel you to take a stand and to provide an atmosphere in which you are most productive. As you prepare your personal philosophy for life and ministry, you should list the values that motivate and empower you, and that are essential to fulfilling your personal mission.

Examples of values:

Faith in God	A Relationship with God
Integrity	Family
Friendships	Prayer

The values listed above may not necessarily be your core values. You need to know what is important to you and defines who you are. As a Christian, there are fixed values that govern how we live our lives. However, occasionally, we meet similar challenges in life with different responses. Of course, the solutions should be biblically sound and reflective of who we are, but they are not always going to be the same.

An example of two people challenged with the same issue, but different values, was Ruth and Orpah in the Scriptures (See Ruth 1). When Naomi informed Ruth that her sister-in-law, Orpah, was returning to her people and her gods, she encouraged Ruth to go also. Ruth chose to stay with Naomi while Orpah returned home. There is no indication that Orpah was wrong for making the decision to leave Naomi, or that her values were less honorable. She just prioritized her values differently. It was more important to Ruth to maintain her relationship with Naomi, while it was more important for Orpah to return to her family. Each of them did what was essential to fulfilling their mission.

Goals. Finally, listing measurable short and long-range goals that will help you grow and accomplish your mission is necessary. Ask yourself what you will accomplish in the next three months or the next year. What specific goals will take you to where you ultimately want to go? Know what the necessary resources are for accomplishing your goals (i.e., technology, finances, mentoring, etc.) Know what you need to get the job done.

Included in listing your goals should be your list of potential obstacles. Name the things that might keep you from reaching your goal(s). Be specific and honest with yourself. One obstacle may be self. If you are fearful and lack confidence, admit that is a potential obstacle. Consider that others may be potential obstacles. The lack of finances may also hinder you from reaching your goal, but awareness and complete honesty is imperative. The bottom line is, be realistic about your mission and ministry. Don't plan with blinders on! Broaden your scope so that there is a strategy in place for dealing with potential obstacles.

Reflection

It isn't enough to say, "I've been called to the ministry!" What have you been called to do? Who have you been called to minister to?

_____

_____

_____

_____

What are some of the obstacles you may encounter?

_____

_____

_____

_____

Prayer: Lord, help me to focus on my assignment and to develop a process for accomplishing your will for my ministry.

Chapter Five

Take the Risk

"Conquering any difficulty always gives one a secret joy, for it means pushing back a boundary-line and adding to one's liberty."
_____*Henri Frederic Amiel*

The Book of Esther is a book about a woman who took a risk. Esther literally risked her life for her people. She had favor as the queen, even though she had only known a life of bondage because of her race. She had grown up in obscurity, but she became a woman of prominence and influence. When she was approached with a request from Mordecai, her uncle, to go to the king on behalf of God's people, she made her reservations known. She was clear about the fact that even as queen, she had limitations. She was not permitted to go before the king unless she was summoned.

Mordecai would not back down. He was determined that this was the only way that their people would be saved. Esther was the one! She had arrived at her place of prominence for this purpose. Ultimately, Esther was persuaded to make the choice to give up her right to live in order to save her nation from death. It was against the law to go before the king without having been first summoned, but she decided to take that chance. Esther did not know if she would survive, but she chose to go before the king with her petition.

How powerful! Esther had enough confidence in herself and her purpose to do what was absolutely against the culture of that time. The other significant thing about this story is that her uncle pushed her into her destiny! They actually portrayed successful teamwork between a male and a female. Mordecai had no reservations about encouraging Esther. Esther's gender was not the issue, saving his people was. What a lesson to be learned from Mordecai. What difference does it make whom God uses, as long as His people are saved?

You may be hindered by your culture (church tradition), but that cannot be your excuse for not doing what you have been called to do. Unfortunately, women still struggle with issues of inequality in the church, as much as any place else, but therein lies the challenge to go and to do what God has called you to do. You were called for this time. What will you do about it? Esther chose to risk her life to deliver her people. She did not make the assignment about herself. It was clearly about her nation. Esther was not sure that her decision to talk to the king would be successful, but she had to try. Because she took that risk, the king responded favorably to her request and elevated her in the nation. Esther impacted the entire Jewish nation, not just in ancient times but even until today! The king gave Esther and Mordecai per-mission to *write a decree concerning the Jews as you please, in the king's name, and seal it with the king's signet ring....* (See Esther 8:8).

The decree gave the Jews permission to fight back should they be attacked by anyone. And then he granted them a special time of celebration called the Feast of Purim. An entire nation was saved and given a holiday because Esther said, "I will go." That's a fierce girl!

Consider the Samaritan women who met Jesus at a well. She came with her pots at a certain time of day expecting that she would be alone. She certainly did not expect to find a Jewish man there, asking her for a drink of water. This woman knew that Jews and Samaritans did not share eating and drinking receptacles, so she was amazed that Jesus would ask her for water. After conversing with Jesus, the Samaritan learned that He knew all about her several husbands. She was convinced that Jesus was a prophet and left her waterpot at the well to return to her town. Now, the risk for this Samaritan woman was to return to the place where her reputation for having many men was known, and to tell the men in that city, *Come, see a Man* . . . . (See John 4:7-29) Why should they care about her announcement about another man? The Samaritan woman did not allow her past to keep her from talking about Jesus. She risked being rejected and judged, but she had been transformed. It was that transformed woman who became a great evangelistic influence for the Samaritans in her town. John 4:39 says, *And many of the Samaritans of the city believed in Him because of the word of the woman who testified, "He told me all that I ever did."*

The Syrophoenician woman whose daughter was demon possessed pushed back several boundary lines to get what she needed. (See Matthew 15:21-28) She was a gentile, which meant she was outside the covenant of Israel. She was a woman. Women were considered to be inferior to men, and no Middle Eastern man would be seen speaking to a woman in public. Lastly, the disciples were frustrated by her presence. And finally, it appeared that Jesus was ignoring her when He did not answer her. (See Matthew 15:23) Rather than walk away and give up on her request, this woman was persistent and determined to risk her own dignity for her daughter's deliverance. She did not allow where she came from to stop her, nor did she allow what the disciples thought of her to stop her. By ignoring the customs of that ancient time, she risked being humiliated. She took the risk! The result? Jesus answered, and said to her, *O woman, great is your faith! Let it be to you as you desire. And her daughter was healed from that very hour.* (Matthew 15:28)

Mary of Bethany also took a risk in Luke 12. While her sister, Martha, remained in the kitchen preparing food to serve to Jesus, Mary joined the men as they sat at the table. Again, according to the custom, women were not to be seen conversing with men. Mary not only joined the men at the table, but she took an expensive ointment and anointed Jesus' feet. Judas was infuriated by this one act because the ointment was so costly. He pretended to be concerned for the poor, and suggested that Mary was being wasteful. His interest was self-serving, at best, as he attempted to minimize what Mary had done. But Jesus spoke up on her behalf and said, *Let her alone; she has kept this for the day of my burial.* (John 12:7)

In each of these stories the woman risked serious consequences to accomplish a particular mission. I believe these women would say today, that it was a chance worth taking. Esther saved her people; the Samaritan woman saved her city; the Syrophoenician saved her daughter, and Mary prophetically anointed our Savior's body for burial. When you are aware of the advantages and possibilities of jumping over hurdles, pushing past obstacles, and doing the extraordinary, you will take the risk.

Reflection

What risk have you taken in ministry and what was the outcome?

_____

_____

_____

_____

How does the outcome of taking a risk impact your ministry?

_____

_____

_____

_____

Prayer: Lord, teach me to trust you more. Help me to overcome my fears and reservations. Help me to face the challenges and even the barriers that might cause me to withdraw.

Chapter Six

Know Before You Go

"An investment in knowledge always pays the best interest."
_____*Benjamin Franklin*

I n my tradition, which is the African-American Pentecostal Church, education has not always been a priority for those called to ministry. Our early fathers promoted the idea that a clean life and a call was all that was necessary to teach and preach the Gospel. Some leaders even condemned a seminary education by suggesting that all one needed to preach the Gospel was a Bible. Growing up, I can remember hearing preachers make remarks about seminaries, calling them cemeteries; as if they had had a slip of the tongue. And so, even though there may be many students of the Word in the Pentecostal tradition today, the spirit and attitude of our early fathers still impacts the thinking of gifted and talented ministers in the church. They find it unnecessary to increase their knowledge in the academic community.

On the other hand, there are denominations that have strict requirements for ministers who expect to lead or obtain ordination. But the reality is that many individuals have separated themselves from the traditions of denominations and have become independent. Many have started new organizations in an attempt to avoid traditionalism, thereby not requiring any formal training for those who acknowledge a call to ministry.

It is not my intention to force the idea of a seminary education on anyone. Although I have attended seminary, I will admit that seminary study alone does not necessarily equip one for the preaching ministry. The call and the gift are significant. However, study and training are absolutely imperative if you are going to be well equipped to preach. Paul instructed Timothy, *Study to show yourself approved unto God.* (See 2 Timothy 2:15) The emphasis should be placed on "study". You must know before you go.

Women in the ministry cannot afford to ignore the discipline of study and training for the purpose of ministering effectively. The struggle to find affirmation in the Body of Christ is huge for so many women in ministry. Yet, there is one thing you can do for yourself that not only empowers you, but it demands respect and honors God. Study!

I like to think of this aspect of ministry as "improving my serve". If I am going to serve the people of God, I want to be at my best. I remember clearly when I acknowledged my call to ministry and my request to God. I told Him, "Now that I have said yes, I need You to help me. Show me what I need to do so that I don't embarrass you, my husband, or myself." That help for me was an education.

Seminary may not be for everyone, but that is not an excuse for not preparing oneself for ministry. We are living in the 21st century. That means that a large number of the people we will minister to are likely to have some higher level of education. We cannot afford to disregard the significance of being prepared to minister effectively.

Effective ministry produces results. It is active and current, and makes a favorable impression. The impression I am referring to is what stays in the minds of our listeners. It is the imprint or the stamp we leave with them. That impression cannot be more about our skills than it is about our information. Wisdom, knowledge and understanding are necessary for us if we are to make the favorable impression concerning God's Word to His people.

Proverbs 2:3-5 says, *If you cry out for discernment, and lift up your voice for understanding, if you seek her as silver, and search for her as for hidden treasures; then you will understand the fear of the Lord, and find the knowledge of God.* We must be intentional about our development. Our attainment of wisdom, knowledge and understanding is like going after a treasure. When we deliberately go after it, God endorses our efforts and makes His Words known to us.

There are several women of wisdom in the Scriptures. One unnamed woman had a significant impact on her nation because of her wisdom. She was known solely as "a wise woman". Nothing else stood out about her, except her wisdom. This woman is found in 2 Samuel 20:16. The story synopsis is that Joab was about to destroy an entire city to catch one man. He and his men were attempting to tear down the walls of Abel when the wise woman of Abel shouted, *"Listen! Listen! Tell Joab to come here so I can speak to him.* (See 2 Samuel 20:16) When Joab came to her, she reminded him that they were *the peaceful and faithful in Israel.* She continued, *You seek to destroy a city and a mother in Israel. Why would you swallow up the inheritance of the Lord?* Paraphrasing, Joab said that was not his intention, but that he only wanted the man that had raised his hand against the king. The wise woman went to the people urging them to act, and they cut off the head of the enemy and threw it out to Joab.

(See 2 Samuel 20:19-22) Innocent lives were saved and Joab got what he wanted.

Wisdom, knowledge and understanding do make a difference. We must look for ways to enhance the gifts that God has given us. Every good gift comes from above, but we should not assume that there is nothing more required of us. Enhancing, refining, or adding to what has been given to us is expected. We find an example of this in Matthew 25:14-30, where a man gave his servants talents (coins) before leaving to take a trip. He distributed the talents according to each person's ability. To one he gave five talents, to another he gave two, and to the last one he gave one. The one with five doubled his money, and so did the servant with two. The servant with one talent did not do any-thing to improve on what he had. Instead, he hid it and told his master that he was giving back to him what had been given. The master said: *You wicked and lazy servant, you knew that I reap where I have not sown, and gather where I have not scattered seed. So you ought to have deposited my money with the bankers, and at my coming I would have received back my own with interest.* (Matthew 25:26-27)

The servants who added to what they received were commended for doing well and promised more. The servant who hid his talent wasn't given anything, as a matter of fact, what he did have was taken away from him and given to the one that had the most. The message here is that if you don't add to the gift that has been given to you, you will lose it! And not only will you lose it, but the gift will be given to someone else. Imagine that! Imagine someone who is already gifted, knowledgeable and prepared to minister being given your gift too, just because you did nothing to add to what God gave you.

Whatever you are called to do, seek to find a way to make it the best assignment it can be. Increase your knowledge in whatever area of ministry you will work in. In so many instances, women are already at a disadvantage. Let's not make our situation any more difficult than it has to be because we are not prepared.

Reflection

What can you do to enhance or increase what has been given to you?

_____

_____

_____

_____

What will you do to ensure that this enhancement takes place?

_____

_____

_____

_____

Prayer: Lord, give me the determination and the wisdom to pursue all that is necessary to be prepared for ministry in the 21st century. Increase my knowledge so that I may minister effectively to an informed society.

Chapter Seven

Remembering Those Who Paved The Way

"We stand on the shoulders of some powerful women."

_____*Sabrina J. Ellis*

Luke 24:1 points out to us that the women who came with Jesus to Galilee were the first to be at the tomb the morning of the Resurrection. The text says, *Now on the first day of the week, very early in the morning, they and certain other women with them, came to the tomb bringing the spices which they had prepared.* These women arrived at the tomb before the expected time of arrival at a cemetery. One could say they were premature by showing up so early in the morning, but the reality is that by showing up early they became primary to the Resurrection story. By being there early, they put themselves in the position of being at the beginning of the most significant event in the history of Christianity.

Secondly, they came prepared. They brought spices *which they had prepared.* They were attempting to make their contribution to the finalization of the embalming process, according to Jewish custom. But as noble as their attempt was, Jesus had been anointed already. The Books of Matthew, Mark and John tell us of the woman who took costly oil and *anointed the feet of Jesus, and wiped His feet with her hair.* (See Matthew 26:6-13, Mark 14:3-9, John12:1-8) Although she was criticized for wasting such valuable oil, Jesus spoke in her defense and vindicated her. Jesus said, *For in pouring this fragrant oil on My body, she did it for My burial.* (Matt. 26:12) The message here is that someone has gone before us.

As good as our intentions and our preparation may be, we cannot afford to disregard those who have paved the way for women in ministry. Let's remember . . .

- Jarena Lee (1783-1850), the first preaching woman of the African Methodist Episcopal Church of America, was allowed by Bishop Richard Allen to preach and was licensed but was refused ordination.
- Isabella Baumfree (1797-1883) took the name Sojourner Truth in 1843, believing this to be the instruction of the Holy Spirit and became a traveling preacher (the meaning of her new name).
- Julia Foote (1823-1900) was the first woman to be ordained a deacon (1894) and the second to be ordained an elder (1900) in the African Methodist Episcopal Zion Church.
- Amanda Matthews-Berry Smith (1837-1915) Born into slavery, she won her freedom from slavery as a result of her preaching ability. She began preaching in 1870 and continued with tremendous success despite cruel racism and barbarous sexism. Although she had only three months of formal schooling,

Smith was both highly articulate and won-derfully anointed. (*The Century of the Holy Spirit*, Synan, 2001)

* Ida B. Robinson (1891-1946) was the founder, first Senior Bishop and President of the Mount Sinai Holy Church of America, Inc. Robinson formed the organization in response to her vision and Divine Call to secure an organizational home where women preachers would be welcomed and encouraged. She withdrew her congrega-tion from the United Holy Church because it denied women the office of bishop. (*The Century of the Holy Spirit*, Synan, 2001)

* Bishop Violet Fisher (1939 -) called to be an evangelist, began preaching at the age of 16. She is the first African-American woman to be elected to the episcopacy in the Northeast Jurisdiction of the United Methodist Church.

These are only a few of the women who blazed the trail for women in ministry. Just as the woman who anointed Jesus for burial prior to His death, these women prepared the way for those of us who have been called to preach, teach, or evangelize. Even though the women showed up at Jesus' tomb that early Sabbath morning to anoint Him with spices, it was not necessary because it had already been done. The women who have gone before us were just as bold and tenacious as the woman in Matthew 26. So, we stand on their shoulders as we pour out the oil from our alabaster boxes.

Epilogue

You do not have to defend your message! Just deliver it! If God said go, GO! It doesn't matter what your past looks like. It doesn't matter what you used to do. It doesn't matter where you came from or what people think about you. You are the only one that can respond to *your* call. But if you fail to answer, God will call and use someone else. Don't allow doubt and the lack of confidence to get in your way.

Once I became confident in myself and what God has called me to do, I was no longer intimidated by those who did not believe. So, I did not waste any more time trying to convince anyone. My focus turned to preparing myself for my assignment. For me, that preparation included an education and a process of spiritual formation. The further I went, the more God confirmed for me that He had indeed called me "for such a time as this". It is imperative for you to know what your calling is and to plan and prepare for that call. An anointing is wonderful, but it works skillfully with information and transformation.

Finally, when you tell your story, tell it with joy! Tell it with gladness. Jesus instructed the women who discovered He was not in the tomb to "Rejoice!" The Bible says, *So they went out quickly from the tomb with fear and great joy, and ran to bring His disciples word.* (Matthew 28:8) No matter what your assignment is, don't forget to rejoice and to worship. Wherever you go, rejoice and worship. And remember, *that He which hath begun a good work in you will perform it until the day of Jesus Christ.* (See Philippians 1:6) Get ready to tell the story!

AFTERWORD

When Sabrina prepared to write her first discussion on this matter of *"women in ministry"*, it was intended for our congregation and designed to discuss the Resurrection of our Lord. Sabrina asked me if she could arrange the Sunrise Service and use some of the sisters to enact some scenes which might have taken place on that morning back in A.D., 33. I agreed. Later in the preparation period, she told me that she would like to name the event; *AND THE WOMEN CAME FIRST.*

So, I came to church on that Easter Sunday morning, Reverend Dr. Sabrina Joyce Ellis stood in the Pentecostal Pulpit at University Circle in Cleveland, read her texts and announced her subject: *AND THE WOMEN CAME FIRST.* It was a blast! During and after the sermon, I enjoyed watching positive change in the people who were exposed to the message that day.

I've enjoyed her careful and respectful treatment of the Scriptures in this matter because this writer worked hard to avoid the usual traps of arrogance, over-defensiveness, and needless rebuke of her male counterparts. Her gentle hand and thoughtful management of every sentence makes us read her treatise as one would read an informational from a friend and beloved sister. Sabrina teaches but never tries to chastise those who may disagree with or fail to understand her positions. She has simply placed information at our disposal and left it to us to ponder.

Sabrina and I share life, love family and ministry, and over the three decades that I've been blessed to be her husband, pastor and *first* teacher I have become richer and much more sensitive to Christ and His call to His daughters in the world. My hope is that our brothers will find this to be another helpful tool for opening the male-dominated room for other called and chosen daughters who have a genuine Word from the Lord.

I am proud of her work and scholarship and always enjoy the challenge that she brings to my own ministry and life. I support her sojourn and conclusions especially in this matter of women in ministry.

Saint Paul is not here with us in this twenty-first century, but his first century admonition was written so succinctly that one should have very little trouble understanding God's intention regarding a surrendered life. I believe that his note to the Galatian church settles it all, *There is neither Jew nor Greek, there is neither bond nor free, there is neither male nor female: for ye are all one in Christ Jesus.* (Galatians 3:28) In other words, *there is no race difference, there is no class difference; and there is no gender difference, in Christ Jesus, for we all are one.*

BISHOP J. DELANO ELLIS, II, D.D.

METROPOLITAN

THE JOINT COLLEGE OF PENTECOSTAL BISHOPS

References

Kise, J., Stark, D., Hirsh, S. (1996). Life Keys. Bloomington, MN: Bethany House publishers.

McKenzie, V. (1996). Not Without a Struggle. Cleveland, OH: The Pilgrim Press.

McMickle, M. (2010). Deacons in Today's Black Baptist Church. Valley Forge, PA: Judson Press.

Synan, V. (2001). The Century of the Holy Spirit. Nashville, TN: Thomas Nelson.

APPENDIX I

Sermon
Matthew 28:8
Don't Let Fear Stop You

So they went out quickly from the tomb with fear and great joy, and ran to bring His disciples word. (Matthew 28:8)

We have just come out of the Easter Season, so this passage and similar passages in the Gospels are fairly fresh on our minds. This portion of the Easter Story is absolutely significant to the Christian Church because it reveals the resurrection of Jesus Christ. I don't necessarily have an Easter sermon for you this morning, but allow me to revisit the dramatic scene (or scenes) that the Gospels provide for us concerning the death, burial and resurrection of Jesus to make my point.

I want to talk about the women in this text who went to the tomb on a Sabbath morning expecting to find Jesus there. Matthew tells us of two women who went to the tomb that morning. But when we read the other Gospels and harmonize the texts, we discover that there were other women who arrived with these two Mary's at the tomb, in hopes of completing the burial process. They went to the tomb expecting to anoint Jesus' body with spices, but He was not there.

Now, we can get extremely excited about the verses prior to our text, because these verses are the foundation of our Christian faith. The angel said to the women, *Do not be afraid, for I know that you seek Jesus who was crucified. He is not here; for He is risen, as He said.* (Matthew 28:5) And even though that's not necessarily my message this morning, it is a good reason to give God a praise!

I want to talk about these women who "*went out quickly from the tomb with fear and great joy.*" They were afraid, yet they had joy! . . . .

They are leaving the tomb with what appears to be opposing emotions. *"They went with fear and great joy."* This is an expression with contradictory words. It is what we call an oxymoron. *"They went with fear and great joy!"* How can this be? How can one be afraid and full of joy at the same time? How can one be scared and joyful at the same time? These emotions are very different. Fear usually consumes and restricts. Fear stops and delays. Fear procrastinates. Fear is distressing and it is aroused by impending danger, evil, or pain; whether the threat is real or imagined. Yet, these girls **went** with **fear and great joy**! I'm wondering this morning if anybody here has ever been afraid! I want to talk to the scared folk! I want to help somebody that doesn't mind admitting; there have been some issues in life to trigger the emotion of fear. No matter how you tried to be brave, no matter how you tried to keep the situation under control, no matter what you did, ultimately, you were just plain old afraid!

It would have been enough for the women in our text to be afraid about Jesus not being in the tomb, but there were some other things that had to have contributed to their fear. Consider all that they had witnessed as they walked with Jesus and supported Him all the way to the cross. They watched their friend and deliverer as He was accused of crimes He did not commit. They watched as He was beaten and hung on a cross for crimes He did not commit. As they watched, they must have been concerned for their own lives because they had been seen with Jesus. (I'm talking about fear!) Walk with these women for just a moment. What were they feeling and thinking as they watched as a friend was brutally murdered? Matthew's gospel confirms that they were there, "looking on from afar."

They heard the voices of those who mocked Him saying, "He saved others; Himself He cannot save. If He is the King of Israel, let Him now come down from the cross, and we will believe Him." They were there. They witnessed the earth quake and rocks split after Jesus commended His Spirit to His Father. They heard the centurion confess, "Truly this was the Son of God!" They were afraid! Apprehension, dismay, dread, terror, horror and trepidation would have been the order of the day. I submit to you that these women may have even been traumatized over these series of events. They were afraid!

But as if that was not enough, when they arrived at the tomb to make their contribution to the embalming process, they experienced another earthquake! The Bible says, . . . *an angel of the Lord descended from heaven, and came and rolled back the stone from the door, and sat on it* . . .(Matthew 28:2) Now, you can't tell me that's not scary! They are in the cemetery! They see an angel that has been introduced by an earthquake! They had already experienced an earthquake three days earlier, with dead folks getting up out of the grave. Now here they are in the cemetery, where things should be pretty quiet, and there is another earthquake and an angel sitting on the stone that has been rolled away from the tomb of Jesus. (I'm still talking about fear!) This angel's face looked like lightning and his clothes were as white as snow! This was a scary thing! So much so, the soldiers guarding the tomb passed out! They couldn't take it!

These women had experienced several things that caused them to be afraid. A crucifixion! Earthquakes and angels! A sealed tombstone rolled back; Roman guards falling out as if they were dead. This was a lot to comprehend, and yet there was something more! *Come on into the tomb and see where they laid His body! Come see for yourself that Jesus is no longer here!* (Paraphrase, Matthew 28:6) I know you were here when His body was wrapped in linen and placed here, but he's not here now! I submit to you that these women may have even been traumatized by the escalating series of events within that three-day period. But in spite of the fear or trauma they had because of their experiences, they had joy! This is amazing to me, you see, because bad experiences can trigger a fear response in us that can be very difficult to suppress. Fear is not something you can just shake off. Fear holds on. Fear tries to stick around. When you are trying to ignore fear, fear makes sure you know it is present.

Fear makes you feel its presence. (Your palms might get sweaty; your face may become pale; your stomach may be upset; you may become anxious; you may become stuck or frozen in a moment of time!) Fear makes its presence known! Yet, the Bible says, *these women went with fear and great joy!* (Matthew 28:8)

Somebody is here today that has been traumatized! Bad experiences have gripped your emotions and caused you to be apprehensive about our tomorrows. You have witnessed some things; you have experienced some things; you have heard some things that keep you from moving forward. But I came to tell you, today, you can still have joy!

IF YOU ALLOW IT, FEAR WILL ROB YOU OF YOUR FUTURE, BECAUSE FEAR IS A FUTURE APPRAISAL EMOTION!

Fear is a future appraisal emotion: although something may have happened to trigger fear, the emotion itself impacts the future. When you are not sure what is **going** to happen, you become fearful of the possibilities; what *might* happen.

• Just a few years ago, my husband was diagnosed with cancer. Five years after the first diagnosis of prostate cancer, he was diagnosed with Chronic Lymphocytic Leukemia . . . I WAS SCARED! The doctors' visits, the treatments, the side effects of the treatment, the prognosis and the possibility of a bone marrow transplant was all nerve racking, to say the very least. Fear was definitely a part of my life. But I decided that I would not complain. I could not afford to let fear stop me. Once I made the decision to "keep it moving", I shared the news of my husband's diagnosis with our congregation.

• When I shared the news that the doctors had given us concerning my husband's health, I said; "The news I have to share with you is serious and even a little scary, but what I want you to do after I give you the information is praise God as if you just received everything you asked Him for." The saying around Pentecostal Church of Christ for the next few years was "pray and praise!" We were determined that we would not just beg God for healing, but we would also praise Him as if He had already healed Bishop Ellis. The end of the story is, that despite our fears, we kept moving and today the Bishop is cancer free!

- The women in the text went, and you can go too! No matter what your fears are, you can go and you can go with joy!

The Death of a loved one; Abuse; Divorce; Abortion; Struggle with cancer; Loss of finances; Murder; Suicide; War; Earthquake; Tornado; Hurricane; Rape; Abandoned by parents; Abandoned by friends . . . WHATEVER it is, you can still have joy!

They went! They had been given instructions to go, and they went! They had to take fear with them, but they went!

You might be afraid, but you can still get up and go; you might be afraid, but you can still move; you might be afraid, but you can still get the job done!

You might have to talk to yourself . . . just tell yourself . . .

I'm going . . . no matter what! **Lack of confidence** can't stop me! **Fear** can't stop me! **Apprehension** can't stop me! **Enemies** can't stop me! I'm going, no matter what! **My bad experiences** can't stop me! **The lies** can't stop me! **What you did to try and stop me** . . . can't stop me! I'm going, no matter what! **And, I'm going with JOY!** I can do this because I have joy! I can make it as long as I have my joy! . . . the joy of the Lord is my strength!

Written by: Dr. Sabrina J. Ellis
Preached at: Pentecostal Church of Christ April 8, 2012
Allen AME Cathedral April 22, 2012

APPENDIX II

Women in Ministry Who Have Impacted My Life

Reverend Dr. Joanne Browning
Ebenezer A.M.E. Church
www.ebenezerame.org

Reverend Dr. Claudette Copeland
New Creation Christian Fellowship
Destiny Ministries
www.claudetteacopeland.org

Reverend Dr. Elaine Flake
The Greater Allen A.M.E. Cathedral
www.allencathedral.org

Women in Ministry Who Have Impacted My Life, continued

Reverend Dr. Cynthia Hale
Ray of Hope Christian Church
Women in Ministry
www.rayofhope.org

Reverend Dr. Jessica Ingram
AMEC Supervisors Council
Women of Hope Project, Inc.

Bishop Cynthia James
Dr. Cynthia James Evangelistic Ministries
www.cynthiajames.org

Reverend Dr. Jacqueline McCollough
Precious Jems Ministries, Inc.
Beth Rapha Bible Institute
www.rizpa.org

Women in Ministry Who Have Impacted My Life, continued

Bishop Vashti McKenzie
First female Bishop in AME Church
www.vashtimckenzie.blogspot.com

Joyce Meyer
Joyce Meyer Ministries
www.joycemeyer.org

Reverend Dr. Susie Owens
Greater Mt. Calvary Holy Church
www.susieowens.org

Reverend Dr. Carolyn Showell
God First Ministries, Inc.
drcdshowell@aol.com

Reverend Dr. Gina Stewart
Christ Missionary Baptist Church
www.christmbc.org

Reverend Dr. Renita Weems
Clergy, Bible Scholar, Author, Coach
www.somethingwithin.com

Dr. Sabrina J. Ellis is the Executive Pastor of the Pentecostal Church of Christ. She received a Master of Divinity degree and a Doctor of Ministry degree from Ashland Theological Seminary in Ashland, Ohio. Dr. Ellis is married to Bishop J. Delano Ellis, II and together they have 6 children and 23 grandchildren.

Contact information:

Pentecostal Church of Christ
10515 Chester Avenue
Cleveland, Ohio 44106
sellispastor@gmail.com

CPSIA information can be obtained at www.ICGtesting.com
Printed in the USA
LVOW082342130912

298720LV00001B/1/P